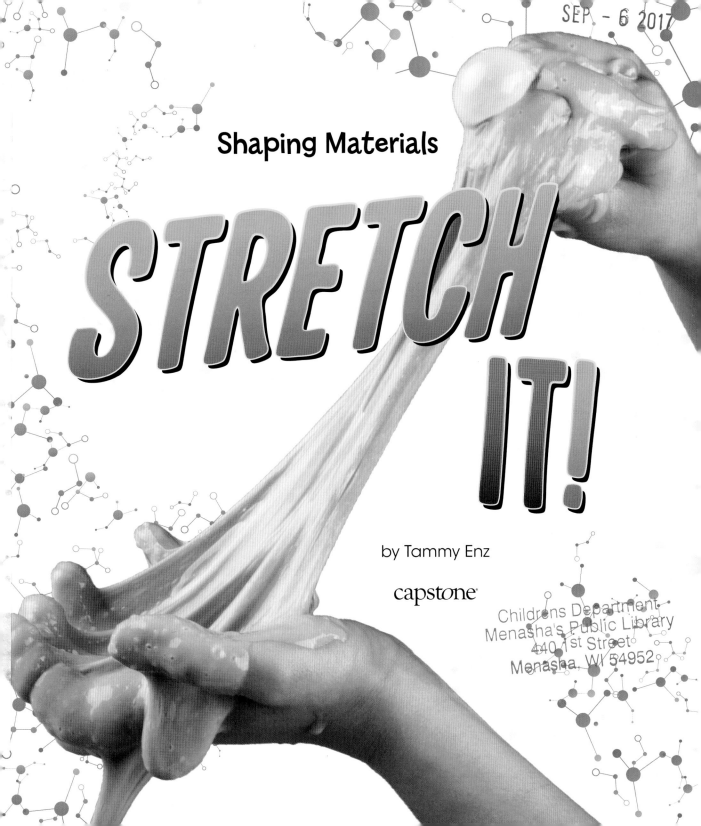

Shaping Materials

STRETCH IT!

by Tammy Enz

capstone

Edited by Linda Staniford
Designed by Kayla Rossow
Original illustrations © Capstone Global Library Limited 2018
Picture research by Kelli Lageson
Production by Victoria Fitzgerald
Originated by Capstone Global Library Ltd

21 20 19 18 17
10 9 8 7 6 5 4 3 2 1

Library of Congress Cataloging-in-Publication Data
Library of Congress Cataloging-in-Publication Data is available on the Library of Congress website.
ISBN: 978-1-4846-4094-4 (library hardcover)
ISBN: 978-1-4846-4098-2 (paperback)
ISBN: 978-1-4846-4103-3 (eBook PDF)

This book has been officially leveled using the F&P Text Level Gradient™ Leveling System.

Acknowledgments
We would like to thank the following for permission to reproduce photographs: Capstone Studio:
Karon Dubke, cover, back cover, 1, 5, 8, 9, 12, 13, 14, 15, 18, 19, 22, (top right and bottom left);
Shutterstock: benjamas11, 20, 22, (top left), Daxiao Productions, 21, Djem, throughout (background),
focal point, 16, Jason Stitt, 6, Lapina, 11, Mark Aplet, 17, N Azlin Sha, 4, 22, (bottom right), Natasha
R. Graham, cover (background), otnaydur, 10, PIMPUN TAWAKOON, back cover, 7

Every effort has been made to contact copyright holders of material reproduced in this book.
Any omissions will be rectified in subsequent printings if notice is given to the publisher.

Printed and bound in China
PO010438F17

Table of Contents

Some words are shown in bold, **like this**.
You can find out what they mean by looking
in the glossary.

What Stretches?

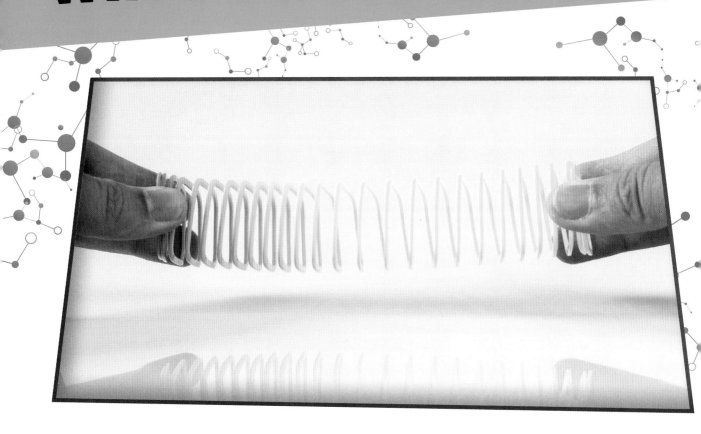

When you pull something, you **stretch** it. Materials that stretch get longer when pulled. You can see a **spring** get longer when you pull it.

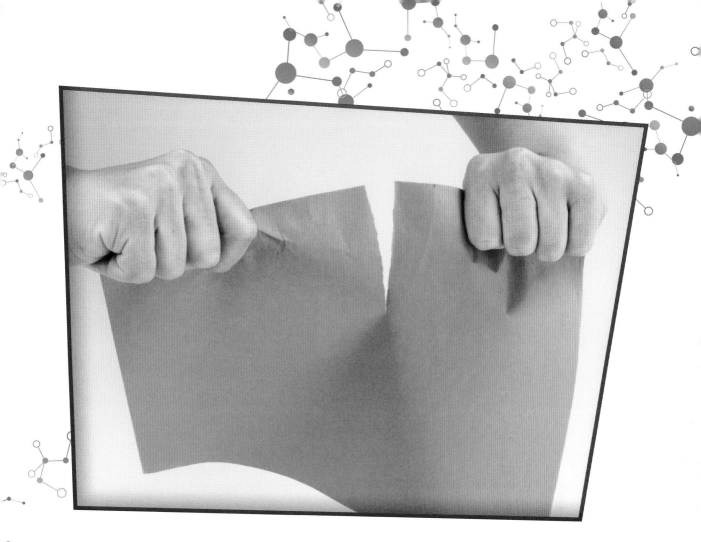

Springs snap back when stretched.
Cotton doesn't stretch much.
Paper tears if you try to stretch it.

Materials That Spring Back

Some materials **stretch** and **spring** back. They are called **elastic**. Things like wool or cloth stretch a little. Then they spring back.

But rubber can stretch twice its
length before springing back.

Project: Bungee Jumper

Rubber is super-**stretchy**. Check it out with this project.

You Will Need:

- Plastic water bottle with cap
- Water
- Permanent marker (optional)
- Rubber bands (several of different sizes)
- Scissors

What To Do:

1. Draw a face on the bottle (optional).
2. Fill half full of water.
3. Cut a rubber band open.
4. Screw one end of the band tightly onto the bottle with the cap.
5. Hold the other end at the edge of a table.
6. Push the jumper off.
7. How far does it fall before it bounces back?
8. Try different water levels. Try different rubber band sizes.
9. Make the jumper almost touch the floor before it bounces back.

Materials That Stretch and Stretch

Not all **stretchy** materials are **elastic**. Some stretch and stretch. But they don't spring back. They break.

Have you ever stretched
bubble gum or caramel?
These things are very stretchy.
But they are not elastic.

Project: Stretchy Goo

Try making some super-stretchy goo!
It **stretches** without **springing** back.

You Will Need:

- 1/4 cup (60 mL) liquid starch (for laundry)
- 2–3 drops food coloring
- 1/4 cup (60 mL) white glue
- Mixing bowl and spoon

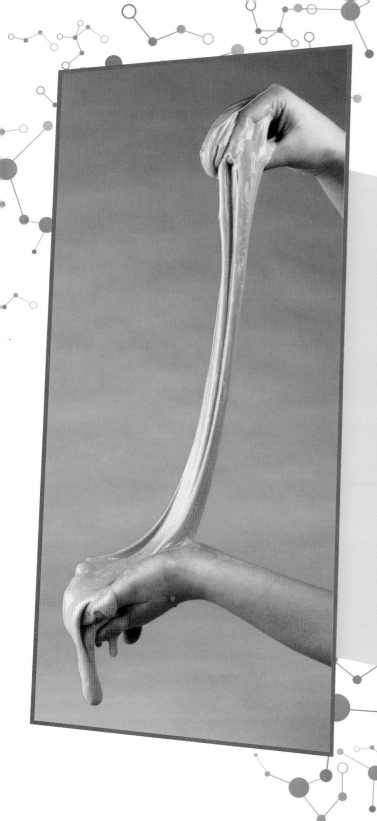

What To Do:

1. Mix the starch and food coloring in the bowl.
2. Add the glue and stir until mixed.
3. Play with and stretch the goo.
4. Notice how it holds its stretched shape.
5. Store the goo in an air-tight container.

Project: Stretchy Caramels

Caramel candies are **stretchy**. But do warm caramels stretch even better? You bet. Try out this project to see how temperature affects stretchiness.

You Will Need:

- 2 caramel candies
- Small microwave-safe bowl
- Microwave oven

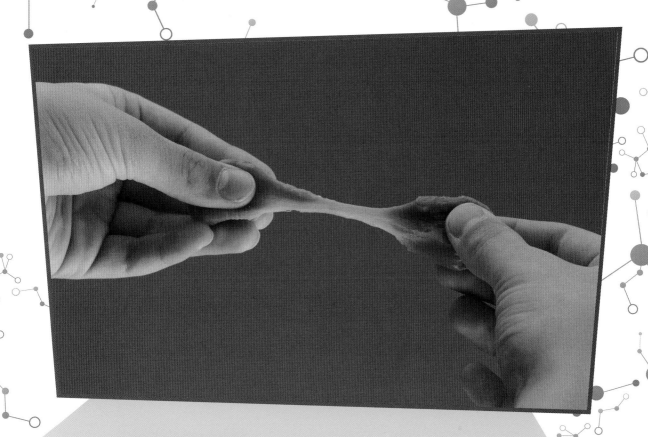

What To Do:

1. Grab one end of a caramel in each hand.
2. Pull to stretch it until it breaks.
3. Place the other caramel in the bowl.
4. Heat it for 10 seconds in a microwave. Have an adult help you.
5. Carefully grab each end and stretch the heated caramel. Does it stretch more easily than the first caramel?

Non-Stretchers

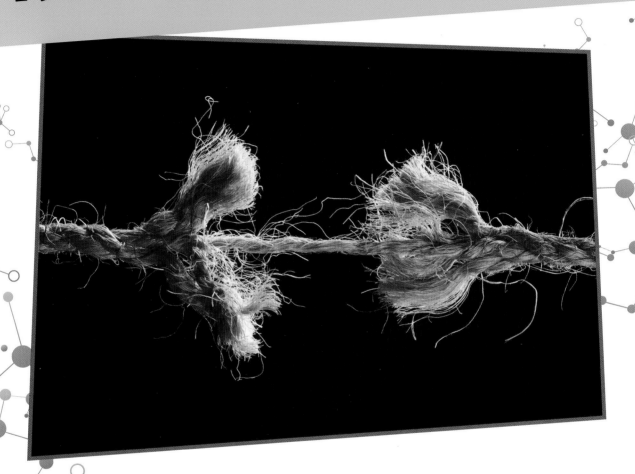

Some materials are hard to **stretch**. They might even break if pulled too hard.

Things that break instead of stretching are called **brittle**. Pull a leaf or a piece of dry spaghetti. These things break. They are brittle.

Project: Spaghetti Pull

Grab some dry spaghetti. Try this challenge with a **brittle** material.

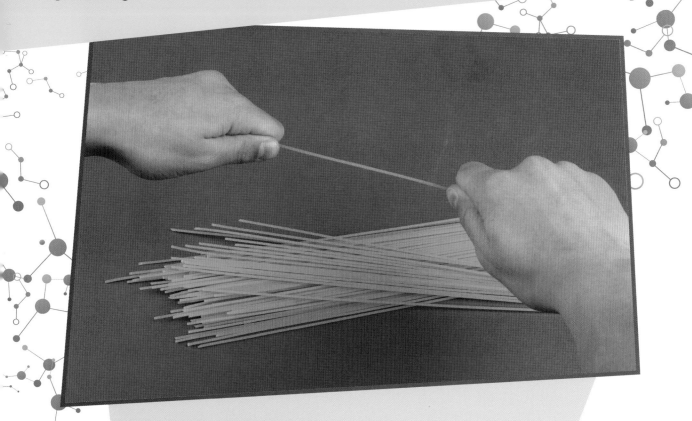

You Will Need:

- 1 package of dry spaghetti

What To Do:

1. Grab one end of a spaghetti piece in each hand.
2. Pull the ends until the spaghetti breaks.
3. Try it again using several pieces.
   Is it harder to pull and break?
4. Keep trying it with more pieces.
5. How many pieces does it take before you can no longer break it?

You Stretch It!

There are lots of **stretchy** things around you. Lots of things you wear or eat are stretchy.

Some of your toys are stretchy too. Find some stretchers. But be careful. Some things are **brittle**. They'll break when stretched!

Picture Glossary

brittle   easy to snap or break

elastic   able to stretch out and return to its original size and shape

spring   something that returns to its original shape after being bent, stretched or pressed down

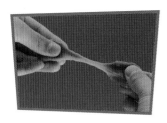

stretch   to make something reach or extend farther

Find Out More

Challoner, Jack. *Maker Lab: 28 Super Cool Projects*. New York, N.Y.: DK, 2016.

Riley, Peter. *Everyday Materials*. Ways into Science. London, U.K.: Franklin Watts, 2016.

Rompella, Natalie. *Experiments in Material and Matter with Toys and Everyday Stuff*. Fun Science. Mankato, Minn.: Capstone, 2015.

Use FactHound to find Internet sites related to this book.

Visit *www.facthound.com*

Just type in 9781484640944 and go!

 Check out projects, games and lots more at **www.capstonekids.com**

Index